CW00369584

ECCLESAL_

Sheffield
City Council

Renew this item at:
http://library.sheffield.gov.uk
or contact your local library

LIBRARIES, ARCHIVES & INFORMATION

216024234

Revised edition, published 2014 by the Guild of St George Publications
10 St Oswald's Road, York YO10 4PF

www.guildofstgeorge.org.uk

ISBN 978-0-9554469-9-3

Updated and printed in England by
Reprotech Studios Ltd, 22 Trinity Lane, Micklegate, York YO1 6EL

RUSKIN at WALKLEY

An Illustrated Guide to the Online Museum

This booklet provides an illustrated guide to *Ruskin at Walkley*, a web project launched in February 2010 as part of a collaboration between the author (formerly a lecturer at the University of Sheffield) and the Guild of St George. The project uses Victorian photographs to reconstruct the appearance of The St George's Museum, a gallery and library founded by John Ruskin in 1875, in the Sheffield suburb of Walkley. Interactive web pages allow visitors to navigate views of the old interior, evoking the way one might move between the rooms of a physical museum. Objects visible in these displays are tagged with 'hotspots', red rectangles that illuminate their outline. These hotspots link to detailed captions and modern images. Presenting the Collection in this way reveals a scheme of display in which copies of works held elsewhere were hung alongside valuable originals. It highlights the Museum's unconventional layout, which can seem strikingly domestic and casual to modern eyes. It registers the role of the Museum furniture, much of which was designed by Ruskin with the aim of displaying objects at the same time as preserving them. And it helps us to appreciate the views and environment Ruskin considered central to promoting what he called 'the liberal education of the artizan'.[1]

Apart from adding to the resources associated with the online museum, the publication of this booklet accompanies the unveiling of the redesigned Ruskin Collection, and the installation of a touch-screen terminal that gives access to the website from the floor of the gallery. This relationship builds on the assistance provided by the Collection's curator, Louise Pullen, in arranging the photography of exhibits, providing captions, and furnishing information for item descriptions. Hosted by the Humanities Research Institute of the University of Sheffield, the completed website is viewable at: **www.ruskinatwalkley.org**

Founding the Museum

Contrary to popular myth, Ruskin never lived in Sheffield. He began thinking of the city after visiting Henry Swan, an engraver and former pupil of his at London's Working Men's College. Swan moved to Sheffield because of the city's reputation for fine metal work, and in that way became acquainted with the hilly suburb of Walkley. Much taken by Swan's new surroundings, Ruskin saw the opportunity for a museum that would meet the needs of local 'workers in iron'.[2] He hoped it would be 'extended into illustration of the natural history of the neighbourhood'.[3] A cottage was purchased for the purpose, and he installed his old student in the role of museum curator.

Ruskin's choice of name for the Museum reflected a longstanding interest in the legend of St George. At the age of just nine or ten years old, he evoked the character of this hero of chivalry in a poem: 'I am the bravest Knight of all', it reads, 'My armour is of gold; / O'er all the field death spreads his pall / When I my wrath unfold.'.[4] Ruskin's fascination with the legend took different forms in later life. In particular, he came to associate breathing fire with industrial smoke, and dragon-slaying with the fight against social injustice. St George was England's patron saint, but also an important figure in the iconography of Venice. Always interested in the links between those two sea-going empires, Ruskin saw St George as a shared object of veneration. He was especially attracted to Vittore Carpaccio's cycle of paintings in the Scuola di San Giorgio degli Schiavoni, noting of Carpaccio's representation that 'His St George exactly reverses the practice of ours', in that 'He rides armed, from shoulder to heel, in proof – but *without* his helmet.'[5] He explains that 'the real difficulty in dragon-fights [...] is not so much to kill your dragon, as to *see* him; at least to see him in time, it being too probable that he will see you first'. We might consider the Museum in this, symbolic, light. It is an attempt to 'see' the dragon first, to take the initiative in the fight to teach better ways of witnessing the world.

The St George's Museum was not meant to be an isolated enterprise. Rather, it was conceived as one element in a wider programme of social reform, to be pursued by a body called The Guild of St George. The Guild had its origins in a Fund established by Ruskin in 1871 for 'the buying and securing of land in England'.[6] The Guild's land was not meant to be 'built upon', but rather 'cultivated by Englishmen with their own hands'.[7] In the following months, Ruskin paid £1000 into the Fund. He then increased his contribution to bonds worth £7000. He did this according to the principle that the Guild's

'Companions' (its members) should donate a tenth of their annual income to its treasury. He intended an analogy with the medieval system of tithes, whereby parishioners gave one tenth of their earnings to the Church. Ruskin initially named the new organization 'The Company of St George'. In 1877, the word 'Company' was replaced by 'Guild', to avoid confusion with profit-making enterprises. Ruskin outlined the Guild's purposes in a series of 'Letters to the Workmen and Labourers of Great Britain' entitled *Fors Clavigera*, a work whose title means among other things 'the strength of the nail bearer'.[8] Ruskin summed up the Guild's impetus as 'simply the purchase of land in healthy districts, and the employment of labourers on the land, under the carefullest supervision, and with every means of mental instruction'.[9] He insisted that this was 'the only way of permanently bettering the material condition of the poor'.

Though Swan's link with Sheffield provided the original impetus for the Museum's location, Ruskin felt obliged to develop more elaborate justifications for his choice of setting. 'Sheffield', he wrote, 'is in Yorkshire, and Yorkshire yet, in the main temper of its inhabitants, old English, and capable therefore yet of the ideas of Honesty and Piety by which old England lived'.[10] The artizanal traditions perpetuated by Sheffield's metal industries were also a source of appeal. According to Ruskin, the 'English work of iron' was 'the only branch of manufacture in which England could even hope to surpass [...] the skill of other countries'. The implication of this observation was that anyone concerned to prompt a revival in craft skills would naturally look first to Sheffield as a site of surviving strength in the practical arts. Ruskin links this strength to the legacy of the North's ecclesiastical foundations. 'Sheffield', he noted, 'is within easy reach of beautiful natural scenery, and of the best art of English hands, at Lincoln, York, Durham, Selby, Fountains, Bolton, and Furness'.[11]

Promoting 'The liberal education of the artizan' meant offering an alternative to the new kinds of professional education developing in the period. Cultivating general intelligence was the priority, not vocational training. All the same, he expected this 'liberal education' to improve standards of craftsmanship, to be professionally beneficial for Sheffield's 'workers in iron'. Ruskin accordingly exhibited works that would evoke the connections between the fine and practical arts. Notable examples in the Collection included Andrea del Verrocchio's 'The Madonna Adoring the Christ Child', and a copy of Botticelli's 'The Virgin and Child with St John', by Charles Fairfax Murray. Ruskin explained that 'Verrocchio was also a great worker in iron', and that Botticelli was 'the greatest Florentine workman', an allusion to the artist's early training as a goldsmith.[12] Working alongside the emphasis on education was an understanding of the

Museum as concerned with preservation. The cottage was used to house what Ruskin called 'Memorial studies' of Venice.[13] These likenesses of Venetian paintings and architectural façades were commissioned from a team of artist-copyists, among them J. W. Bunney, Frank Randal, Thomas Matthews Rooke, Henry Roderick Newman and Charles Fairfax Murray. Work produced by these artists plays an important part in the online reconstruction.

Within walking distance of Sheffield's industrial heart, Walkley nevertheless retained a relationship with the countryside. Parts of the suburb overlooked the pastoral beauty of the Rivelin Valley; and, being on a hill, it benefited from comparatively clean air. Ruskin explained that 'The mountain home of the Museum at Walkley was originally chosen, not to keep the collection out of smoke, but expressly to beguile the artisan out of it'.[14] This reference to a 'mountain home' seems an exaggeration, but it helpfully sets Sheffield in a wider European frame, and recalls Ruskin's early reverence for Alpine landscape, developed first in the 1820s and 1830s whilst touring the Continent with his parents. Nor, indeed, was Ruskin alone in connecting Walkley with mountains. A visiting journalist wrote that the Museum was 'Built on the brow of a hill', in a 'house', that 'overlooks the Rivelin Valley, or rather a series of converging valleys, that in their wild uncultivated beauty are suggestive of the Alps'.[15] The Museum's physical eminence was part of its function. Metal workers from the city were invited to undertake a symbolic ascent, which would take them up the steep hill of South Road, leading to Walkley's upper reaches. Once achieved, their perspective would be altered. No longer overlooking central Sheffield, they would behold instead the greenery of the Loxley Valley and the Rivelin Valley. The reward for the climb would be fresh air, and a sight of Ruskin's art treasures.

A stone extension was built on to the Museum in 1878, to provide additional space for Swan and his family. Signs of this work can be seen in the 'Exterior' photograph, discussed below. A further extension, erected to provide more exhibition space, was opened in May 1885. Ruskin's plans owed much to the classical conception that museums should be 'places of the Muses'. This allowed for the idea that the Museum could exist within and beyond its four walls, interacting with the wider environment in productive ways. The views over the valley, and the gardens in the grounds, all formed part of this broader 'museum'. The Guild of St George bought additional plots of land around the Museum in 1877, 1881, and 1884. This left it standing in close to one acre of land.

An article in *The Daily Graphic* from 1890 offers a colourful account of the cramped conditions. The writer finds the exhibition space 'overflowing, with all manner of precious stones and crystals, old books, and rare missals'.[16] This situation was exacerbated by the ceaseless arrival of new exhibits, and by the residential needs of Swan and his family. Ruskin found ways of justifying the practical limits imposed by the building, even suggesting that the smallness of the space magnified the symbolic power of its contents. It was, he wrote, a space subject to the 'Curator's skilful disposition to contain more than such an apartment ever before contained, accessible to public curiosity'.[17] Yet Ruskin was keen to establish the Museum on a sustainable footing, and he understood that this meant finding, or building, a much larger structure. He initially envisaged an enlargement of the Walkley property, with a separate residence for the curator built on adjoining land. The need for larger premises was such that many objects had to be kept in store. Treasures were said to be left 'lying in lavender'.[18] Ruskin especially regretted that 'casts from St. Mark's, of sculptures never cast before', were 'invisible and useless till I can build walls for them'. In 1880, he used a letter in *Fors Clavigera* to ask the public to help him realize plans for a new building. With 'a working man's Bodleian Library' in mind, he asked the architect E. R. Robson to produce preliminary designs. It was initially proposed that 'the building should be of red brick, faced with the marbles of Derbyshire', but Robson objected that 'neither Derbyshire nor any other marbles would stand in our climate'.[19] He argued for granite instead and quoted an estimated cost of £5000.

Although several sites for the new museum were considered, a piece of land on the Endcliffe Hall estate (West Sheffield) was the focus of attention. The plans for this museum were eventually aborted after a series of delays, and a legal problem that prevented Ruskin vesting the property of the Guild in the hands of the City. Ruskin then turned his attention to land the Guild owned in the Worcestershire locality of Bewdley. This scheme was announced in Ruskin's Report to the Guild of January 1885, in which he invited financial support from the public. He commissioned designs for this museum from the architect Joseph Southall. Drawn up in 1884-6, they can now be seen hanging in The Ruskin Collection. Ruskin's calls for public support did not meet with success, forcing him to abandon this last attempt to open a purpose-built museum.

In 1886, The Corporation of Sheffield (now, Sheffield City Council) bought the Meersbrook estate. A large Georgian house stood on the land, into which Ruskin was invited to move the entire collection. He initially declined this offer because he still hoped to raise sufficient public subscriptions to build a museum to his own plans. The situation changed with Ruskin's declining health. At that time, the Guild's affairs were managed largely by George Thomson, a Huddersfield mill owner, and by George Baker of Bewdley, a former Mayor of Birmingham. Thomson and Baker re-opened negotiations with the Corporation. In 1889, it was decided to accept the Corporation's offer and move the Museum into the mansion at Meersbrook. The Guild agreed to lend the contents to the Corporation for a fixed term. The official opening of the converted building took place on 15 April 1890, and it was widely reported in the national press. A new name came with the Museum's new home: henceforth, it would be known as The Ruskin Museum.[20]

Ruskin at Walkley

The idea of creating a virtual reconstruction originated in my first visits to the Ruskin Gallery (as The Ruskin Collection was formerly called), in 2005. At that time, I was keen to identify possible areas of collaboration between the Collection and the University. I knew that Ruskin House on Bole Hill Road had been the first home of the Museum. But the building's appearance did not seem to tally with the photographs I had seen of the original premises. It surprised me that there was no plaque to commemorate this earlier use, or much information in local guides. Returning to the Gallery, I noticed only the occasional allusion to Walkley in its displays. It seemed important to remind visitors of the Museum's origins in a well-known suburb. I had already noticed the haunting power of the surviving Victorian photographs. Impressive results could be achieved simply by applying a digital zoom. Details that were previously obscure could be made out in this way. Far from dispersing the sense of mystery, enlargements intensified the impression of a window on the past. One could 'explore' these rooms, prying into corners, examining the pattern of wall coverings. At the same time, certain things could not be known, such as the exact source of light projecting from the windows of an extension demolished more than a century ago.

The idea gradually formed of using these photographs as the basis for a reconstruction of the Walkley interiors. In the form of a website, this would allow the project to achieve virtually what could no longer be achieved in real space. I was especially concerned to uncover links between the exhibited objects and the spaces they inhabited. This meant introducing an interactive element to the photographs, whereby visible exhibits were marked with 'hotspots' that could be activated to reveal more information as well as modern images. Photographs of the Museum's exterior could be set alongside other surviving photographs of the area and its views. A further perspective might be achieved through comparison with modern views of the surviving buildings.

I was conscious nevertheless of the difficulties in speaking of 'reconstruction'. If the word was to be meaningful, it needed to admit limitations from the outset. One cannot recover the essence of something that has passed away. 'Reconstruction' in this case had to be something like an interpretative process, a way of bringing evidence to life by generating connections. To avoid passing conjecture off as fact, it would be crucial to present results in the light of an approximation or model. With these limits in place, the project began a process of sceptical reassembly. In broad terms, the task was to answer the practical challenge implicit in Caroline Morley's observation that 'No one but Ruskin […] has ever been in command of the arguments necessary to make the [museum's] various juxtapositions understandable'.[21] The reconstructive efforts of the project were aimed at achieving an understanding of these very 'juxtapositions', though the emphasis would be on the displays themselves rather than the founder's intentions.

Visual reconstruction was not pursued for its own sake; it served instead as an explorative process, a method for identifying connections, and new findings. This necessitated a physical inspection of the property. It had been converted into a 'Girls' Training Home' after it was sold by the Guild, and it was given the name of Ruskin House at that point. Still, it was not clear how this larger property related to the cottage that once housed the Museum, a building whose address had been listed as Bell Hagg Road. I was informed, anecdotally, that there was nothing much to see at Ruskin House. It seemed likely the interior had been heavily converted, with the older rooms 'knocked through' into larger spaces. Without the reconstructive discipline of the project, the need to verify the situation might have felt less pressing. As it stood, I pushed a speculative note through the letterbox of Ruskin House, and hoped for a reply from the landlord. A generous reply came a few weeks later and, excitingly, the offer of a tour.

My first visit confirmed that the cottage in the old photographs was located at the back of what is now Ruskin House, and that its entrance originally served

Bell Hagg Road. When the property was converted, it was entirely re-orientated, with the old cottage serving as just one wing of a much larger structure. What first seemed an unfamiliar exterior turned out to be explicable as the effect of an additional floor. The survival of the Victorian porch confirmed that it remained essentially the same cottage. Even the metal hinges were visible that once supported the Museum's wooden shutters. On entering, I realized that the predicted 'knocking through' had not occurred, and in fact that the original floors (cellar, ground floor and first floor) were still self-contained. With a slightly extended kitchen, the cottage survived as a discrete flat within the wider complex of Ruskin House. I was fortunate to be shown around again in July 2009, when the rooms were no longer occupied. This provided an opportunity to take photographs, to measure dimensions, and to discuss unusual structural features with the manager of the building. This was also a chance to see the bedrooms, and their views over the Rivelin Valley, and Loxley Valley.

A third objective, running alongside reconstruction and exploration, was to create an accessible resource that would appeal to a broad spectrum of people. Teachers and researchers were one obvious target audience. Uses might range from teaching art history to university students, to educating Sheffield school children about local history, or using the reconstructed displays for the purpose originally intended: inspiring students of design and the practical arts. A page would be created where case studies could be reported, so as to provide a source of ideas for future pedagogy. Ensuring that these functions would be compatible with use by the general public was one of the most challenging aspects of the project. My approach was to rely on the broad appeal of the Collection itself, which in its time reached an audience of local people, students, and interested visitors. I hoped to preserve its appeal by ensuring that the reconstructions were always visual at point of entry. Lengthy descriptions would be available, but they would always follow, rather than precede, the more intuitive response that tends to prompt interest. The online habit of 'browsing' seemed an appropriate analogy for the kinds of curiosity the displays originally provoked, and one basis for their continuing appeal.

Project Homepage

The image chosen for the project homepage is an engraving of the Museum exterior, originally published in *Sheffield Illustrated*, a collection of the views published in the *Sheffield Weekly Telegraph* in 1884.[22]

Figure 1. Website homepage, *Ruskin at Walkley: Reconstructing the St George's Museum*

The view was chosen for its welcoming mood, for the way it seems to issue an invitation to enter. Just as readers of the *Sheffield Weekly Telegraph* were drawn to the original Museum, so we are beckoned into the online museum by the convergence of two paths at the cottage's front door. The garden setting and the fruit trees are treated in a Romantic style that establishes a contrast with the detailed photographs used for the interactive displays. An elegant garden gate is visible to the side of the cottage. Three slender trees rise behind it, lending an Italianate mood. On the right-hand side, the style is closer to a controlled wilderness: the path begins in shadow, and an older native tree spreads its branches, its trunk obscured by parasitic vines. Conventional details of this kind indicate that the Museum was not just a building or an institution that existed physically, but also an idea. As this stylised prospect demonstrates, its meaning was susceptible to fashioning and re-fashioning according to the tastes of the day.

Exploring the Online Displays

The homepage is the portal to the online museum. It includes links to resources that develop an understanding of the Museum contents. From here, we can access information on the history of the Museum, on Ruskin, and on the aims of the project. Clicking 'Explore the Museum' allows us to enter the series of online reconstructions. The first page, entitled 'Exterior', shows a view of the cottage by an unknown photographer, with the approximate date, 1886.

Figure 2. 'Exterior' view, *Ruskin at Walkley*; Unknown photographer, c. 1886, Collection of the Guild of St George, Museums Sheffield

As in the engraving, two benches are visible under the ground-floor windows, and the Museum's rear extension stretches behind the cottage. The same trees are in view, though it is winter, and their leaves have fallen. Notwithstanding the softening effect of the ivy growing up the porch, the overall impression is harsher than the engraving, and indeed more in keeping with the area's bricky austerity. In common with the other online displays, the cursor can be passed across different sections of the photograph to illuminate hotspots. These may, in turn, be activated with a mouse click. In this case, the cursor is resting on the porch, causing the hotspot for that part of the building to light up.

'Interior' View

The interactive features of the 'Exterior' photograph are better appreciated once we have seen the interior displays. These are based on Victorian photographs whose level of detail is sufficient to show the original hanging position of dozens of exhibits. With the aid of digital zoom, and some detective work, it

The Blacksmith's Forge
Benjamin Creswick (1853-1946).
Terracotta relief, 1870s

Figure 3. 'Interior' view, *Ruskin at Walkley*; Unknown photographer, c. 1887, Collection of the Guild of St George, Museums Sheffield

was possible to identity nearly every object. Sometimes, the shape of a picture frame disclosed the identity of a work without other distinguishing features. Passing the cursor over objects reveals thumbnail images in colour; clicking them reveals a detailed description and an enlarged modern photograph. In this respect they are interactive, at the same time as static. They are static because the photographs have not been animated and, more symbolically, because the displays are locked in time: visible, but forever out of reach. The tendency of many online resources is to incorporate animation and 360 degree moving perspectives. By maintaining simplicity, *Ruskin at Walkley* avoids the visual distraction of an overly 'busy' interface. Equally, it is important to understand that this is not a searchable database, or a comprehensive online catalogue. Instead of locating a specific item about which one has foreknowledge, the displays foster an explorative approach.

Clicking the link named 'Interior' on the homepage reveals a photograph of the small room in the original cottage (figure 3). Prior to the construction of the rear extension, it served as the Museum's sole exhibition space.

Prints are propped for temporary display on the mantelpiece and on other available surfaces. Works of art hang from the walls; books are piled on shelves in free-standing cabinets; and, in the bottom left-hand corner, one can just make out the edge of a display case, probably for minerals. While the clutter reflects a determined arrangement of objects in view of the camera's lens, there is also something convincingly Ruskinian about the scene: a sort of cabinet

of curiosities, verging on bric-a-brac, with a hint of the vicarage library.

The cursor in the screenshot is resting on an object that sits at the centre of the mantlepiece. With the hotspot illuminated, a thumbnail appears showing a detail of the object, and its identity, *The*

Figure 4. Benjamin Creswick, The Blacksmith's Forge, Terracotta relief, 1870s, Collection of the Guild of St George, Museums Sheffield

Blacksmith's Forge, a terracotta relief made by Benjamin Creswick (figure 4). One mouse click opens a page of detailed description of the work and the artist's biography. From this, we learn that the story of Creswick is also the story of the Museum and its founding principles. As a local workman with no prior experience of art education, he was the kind of visitor Ruskin was hoping to attract. In their *Library Edition* of Ruskin's works, Cook and Wedderburn tell the story of how Creswick, as a 'young grinder', 'strolled one Saturday afternoon into the Museum.', and 'fell into conversation with the curator'.[23] 'The spark was quickened,' they explain, 'and the grinder became a sculptor.' There is something of the Evangelical conversion experience to this account: the lighting of a spark that prompts a larger transformation. Creswick succeeded in becoming a professional artist, eventually taking up the post of model-master at the Birmingham School of Art. Clicking on the image opens an enlarged version.

In *The Stones of Venice*, Ruskin spoke of the 'fatal error of despising manual labour when governed by intellect'.[24] Creswick pays homage to an ideal union of the mind and body. The muscles of the blacksmith expend brute force, but it is force guided by skilful handling of the hammer, and by intelligent co-

Figure 5. Frank Randal, *'The Entombment of Christ, after Titian*, Watercolour on paper, 1886, Collection of the Guild of St George, Museums Sheffield

operation with a fellow worker. One productive outcome is suggested by the presence of the children in the background, who derive sustenance from the labour of their parents. As in Charles Dickens's *Great Expectations* (1861), the values of the forge are given full artistic attention. The volcanic power of the furnace inspires awe, but its infernal quality is tempered by appreciation of the frank labour relations it inspires. The bond between work and home life, and between labour and its profits, appears to have been restored.

Visible in the bottom right-hand corner of the 'Interior' photograph is *The Entombment of Christ, after Titian*, (figure 5) a watercolour painted in 1886 by Frank Randal (1852-1917).

The object description explains that 'the figures from left to right are: the Madonna, Joseph of Arimathea, St John, Christ and Nicodemus'; but the most crucial feature of this painting is its status as a copy. Speaking of Titian's original in the Louvre, Ruskin had described it as 'The finest Titian in the Gallery, glowing, simple, broad and grand.'[25] He wrote that 'The head of the St John and St Joseph are [...] grand conceptions, and the foliage of the landscape graceful in the extreme.' He identifies in it one of 'the most delicate transitions of colour I remember.' Ruskin made notes in his diary that tell us he was interested in its faults as well as its achievements. '[T]he head of Christ is entirely sacrificed,' he writes, 'being put in the deepest possible shade, against clear sky, and it is disagreeable in itself.' Imperfections in the original sanction the inevitable imperfections of the copy. Such imperfection might include the decision to render the oils of the original in the alien medium of watercolour. The copyist becomes an intermediary between the student and the great work, a stepping-stone between the humble aspirant and a distant ideal of art. The message is one of striving rather than achieved perfection.

The Museum's reliance on copies was in certain respects typical of a tendency in the period to use copies for purposes of art education. In 1867, an international Convention was signed in Paris 'for promoting universally reproductions of works of art for the benefit of museums of all countries'. The South Kensington Museum's collection of plaster casts (now, the Victoria and Albert Museum's) was built up for this purpose. Similarly, engravings were circulated in journals and magazines to allow a mass audience to see works located abroad, or in private collections. For Ruskin, copies were not just useful; they seem to have possessed no stigma at all. They were hung alongside original work without fear of detracting from their value. Such considerations acquire particular importance, and extra complexity, when considered in this online context. The virtual museum, after all, relies on photographic copies of copies. A digital image of Randal's copy is two steps, rather than one, away from Titian's original. Unlike Randal's actual painting, it happens also to be endlessly replicable.

Extension, View 1

We can proceed to the next stage of the online museum by clicking on 'Extension, View 1'. This reveals the first view of the long room that was opened at the rear of the Museum in May 1885. The archives of The Ruskin Collection include a collection of receipts, detailing items of expenditure. Among them is an invoice from Primrose & Co. (Church Street, Sheffield),[26] dated 15 December 1882.[27] At its head are the words 'Eclipse Patent Glazing', and an engraved image of a conservatory. The invoice runs over several pages, detailing expenses ranging from heavy materials such as timber (137 ft), and iron bars, to smaller entries such as 'timber for door', 'lengths of fall pipe', hinges, screws, calamined nails, paint, and joiners' time. A further account, dated 1883, details more work completed by Primrose & Co. It is headed 'Carpenter joiners plumber painter

Western Façade of the Basilica of San Marco, Venice
John Wharlton Bunney (1828-1882). Oil on canvas, 1877-1882.

Figure 6. Detail of 'Extension, View 1', *Ruskin at Walkley*; Unknown photographer, c. 1886, Collection of the Guild of St George, Museums Sheffield

& glaziers work necessary to complete additions and alterations to the Museum in accordance with Mr Swann's [*sic*] instructions and the drawings furnished by us'. The total sum comes to £181 0s 4d. A crude calculation based on the retail price index indicates a construction cost today of £13,600.

Unlike the cottage interior, the extension was evidently a designed space. Paintings and plaster casts could be hung on the wall at three levels. The pillars at the back hint vaguely at the classical dignity of the period's great public museums. The curtained arrangement is reminiscent of a stage-set, while the Corinthian capitals are offset by a border of Venetian Gothic arches and spandrels. A fireplace and coal-scuttle restore the domestic air; meanwhile, the flames of the fire lend the peculiar impression of an altar. Sitting above, like a secular altar-piece, is John Wharlton Bunney's oil painting, *The Western Façade of the Basilica of San Marco* (1877-1882). One of the treasures of the Collection, it was commissioned by Ruskin for the fee of £500 and paid for partly by the St Mark's Fund (1879-1883), established to protect the treasures of Venice from harm. Cook and Wedderburn record that it measured 7 feet 7 inches wide, and 5 feet high, and that 'the artist spent upon it no less than six hundred days' constant labour'.[28] The unusual level of detail reflects the painting's intended function as an accurate architectural record. Having stationed Bunney in Venice for the purpose of 'catching' architectural detail, Ruskin suggested that his drawings 'will become of more value to their purchasers every year, as the buildings from which they are made are destroyed'.[29]

To the immediate right of Bunney's painting is a wooden case containing a plaster cast. Clicking on this object reveals its provenance: recording a

Bird and Grapes

Plaster Cast from the Outer Archivolt of the Central Door, Basilica of San Marco, Venice, 1880s.

Work

This cast is from the outer archivolt of the central door to the Basilica of San Marco. It is categorized under 'Groups of Birds, Fruit, and Leaves'.

It is interesting to compare Ruskin's cast with modern photographs of the archivolt as seen today (bottom right).

Note that the bird in question seems to have lost its head since Ruskin took his plaster cast.

Collection of the Guild of St George, Museums Sheffield

Enlarge Image

Ruskin on Sculpture

The reason for the Museum's emphasis on sculpture is given in Ruskin's 'General Statement Explaining the Nature and Purposes of St George's Guild' (1882):

Modern photograph of archivolt, © Marcus Waithe, 2010

'Sculpture is the foundation and school of painting; but painting, if first studied, prevents, or at least disturbs, the understanding of the qualities of Sculpture. Also, it is possible to convey a perfect idea of the highest quality of Sculpture by casts, and even, in the plurality of cases, to know more of it by a well-lighted cast than can be known in its real situation. But it is impossible to copy a noble painting with literal fidelity; and the carefullest studies from it by the best artists attempt no more than to reproduce some of its qualities reverently, and to indicate what farther charms are to be sought in the original.' (*Works*, 30, p. 56).

Detail of Bird and Grapes, © Marcus Waithe, 2010

Figure 7. Detail of object description for 'Bird and Grapes'; *Ruskin at Walkley*

sculptural study of *Bird and Grapes*, it was taken from the outer archivolt of the central door of St Mark's Basilica, Venice. Sculpture held an important place in Ruskin's wider educational system. In his *General Statement Explaining the Nature and Purposes of St George's Guild* (1882), he wrote that 'Sculpture is the foundation and school of painting; but painting, if first studied, prevents, or at least disturbs, the understanding of the qualities of Sculpture'.[30] It was therefore crucial that his students could access sculpture at the beginning of their education. Ruskin believed it 'possible to convey a perfect idea of the highest quality of Sculpture by casts, and even, in the plurality of cases, to know more of it by a well-lighted cast than can be known in its real situation'. Clicking the hotspot reveals a photographic comparison of the Victorian cast and the surface as it survives today.

Cook and Wedderburn note of the casts from the Doge's Palace, that they were 'made before restorations, so that they are of peculiar value'.[31] In this case, the original has fallen foul of weathering and erosion, rather than insensitive restoration. The Sheffield copy retains something of value lost to the Venetian original: the bird, it would appear, has now lost its head. The sculpture's lofty position above the central door of San Marco also lends weight to Ruskin's suggestion that Victorian students would be better served by casts that could be handled and turned than by the thing itself.

On the table in the foreground of 'Extension, View 1' lies the Museum Visitor Book. It comprises seven volumes of detailed entries, specifying full names and addresses. Many are from the working class districts of Sheffield. The books also record a steady stream of visitors from other cities and sometimes other countries. Taking September 1880 as an example, one finds multiple entries for Benjamin Creswick, who was presumably using the Collection to pursue his artistic ambitions. Other names include Enoch Ward, who signs himself as a student

Table

Unknown maker, probably Sheffield based, Oak, with cloth covering, c. 1875-1885

Examples of the Museum's original furniture still survive.

These include cases for plaster casts, book shelves, and a coin cabinet. Modern curatorial standards, and constraints of space, make it hard to use these items in the modern Ruskin Gallery.

A new use has been found for this table. It is now located at the Guild of St George's recently constructed Ruskin Studio at Uncllys Farm, near Bewdley, Worcestershire.

The fabric insert is based on the Vine wallpaper pattern designed by William Morris in 1873: though rather faded, it is a modern addition, as the original photographs show.

Museum Table, now located at Ruskin Studio, Uncllys Farm, Bewdley, Worcestershire

Detail of Museum Table, now located at Detail of Museum Table, now at Ruskin Studio, Uncllys Farm, Bewdley, Worcestershire

Figure 8. Detail of object description for 'Table'; *Ruskin at Walkley*

from South Kensington Art School, and a whole family bearing the surname of Fox, from 89 Daniel Hill, Walkley: Mary Fox, Tom Fox, Arthur Fox and Lilly Fox. There is an Edith Walker from Leeds, and a Syd A. Gimson from Leicester. Other names include Joseph Ashford Jenkinson, a schoolmaster from Nether Edge, Sheffield, and one J. J. Short from King's College, London. An indecipherable signature from the Bethnal Green Museum, London, indicates contact with figures from other parts of the museum world.

The Visitor Book is sitting on one of the Museum's purpose-built tables. A page of information is devoted to this piece of furniture. (Figure 8)

One of the aims of the online museum is to restore connections between the objects currently on display in The Ruskin Collection, and the physical machinery and atmosphere of the Museum. Though unsuitable for exhibition, the furniture remains historically significant for its connection with Walkley. The tables are now in use at the Ruskin Studio, an education centre located on Uncllys Farm, a Guild property in Bewdley, Worcestershire. After years in store, the tables are now part of the daily work of a Ruskinian institution that combines farming with community work. Close attention to the photographs reveals that they have been re-covered in a woven cloth bearing a William Morris wallpaper design.

Extension, View 2

Clicking on 'Extension, View 2' reveals a view of the room from the opposite direction.

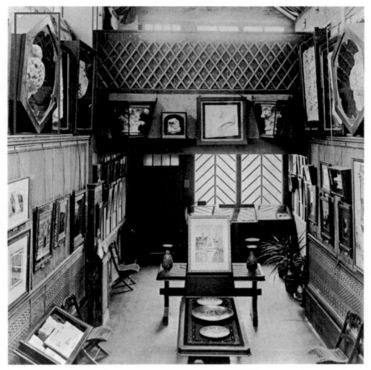

Ornamented Boss
Plaster Cast from the Western
Façade of the Basilica of San
Marco, Venice, 1880s.

Figure 9. 'Extension, View 2', *Ruskin at Walkley*; Unknown photographer, c. 1886, Collection of the Guild of St George, Museums Sheffield

Linear window slats, and the careful arrangement of vases and plants, create a minimal effect, reminiscent of Japanese influence and the Aesthetic style. The minstrels' gallery reflects Ruskin's longstanding attachment to medieval forms in architecture. In this screenshot, the wooden case of an ornamented boss has been selected. The boss is a plaster cast taken from the western façade of the Basilica of San Marco in the 1880s. It represents a further example of the way that a copy can preserve detail now lost from the original object.

Comparing the Victorian cast with the original reveals the boss to be missing three of its encircling vine leaves, as well as the abstract flower pattern at its heart. A Collection that might appear merely antiquarian evidently retains an important secondary role, in that it performs the work of preservation that Ruskin originally envisaged.

Ornamented Boss

Plaster Cast from the western façade of the Basilica of San Marco, Venice, 1880s.

Work

This cast of an acanthus boss is one of ten examples of sculpture from St Mark's that Ruskin described as 'pure thirteenth-century of rarest chiselling' (*Works*, 24, pp. 286-291). For Ruskin, the acanthus bosses were 'the most instructive pieces of sculpture' in the Museum.

Collection of the Guild of St George, Museums Sheffield

Enlarge Image

It is interesting to contrast the detail preserved in Ruskin's cast with the damaged surface of the same boss as seen today on the outer archivolt of the central door of St Mark's.

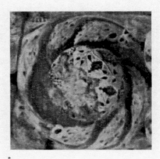

Ruskin on Bosses

Enlarging on the significance of ornamented bosses in *Lectures on Architecture and Painting* (1853), Ruskin asks his reader to 'Imagine the effect on the minds of your children [...if] every boss on your buildings were, according to the workman's best ability, a faithful rendering of the form of some existing animal, so that all their walls were so many pages of natural history' (*Works*, 12, p. 66).

Ruskin extends this principle of education to comment on the conditions of labour: 'And finally, consider the difference, with respect to the mind of the workman himself, between being kept all his life carving [...] repetitions of one false and futile model, -- and being sent, for every piece of work he had to execute, to make a stern and faithful study from some living creature of God'.

Figure 10. Detail of object description for 'Ornamented Boss'; *Ruskin at Walkley*

Extension, View 3

Moving to 'Extension, View 3', we view the room once again in the direction of the fireplace. Unlike 'Extension, View 1', this image picks out the exhibits hanging on the left-hand wall.

'St Ursula and two Maids of Honour, the Moment before Martyrdom', after Carpaccio Charles Fairfax Murray (1849-1919). Watercolour and bodycolour on paper, 1877.

Figure 11. 'Extension, View 3', *Ruskin at Walkley*; Unknown photographer, c. 1886, Collection of the Guild of St George, Museums Sheffield

The highlighted watercolour is by Charles Fairfax Murray, one of Ruskin's team of copyists. It shows a portion of a series of nine paintings by Carpaccio. These paintings tell the story of St Ursula's martyrdom. Their Venetian significance is underlined by their having been completed in tempera for that city's Confraternity of St Ursula. The subject is symbolically important as an example of the way in which Ruskin could mix up artistic associations with the preoccupations of his private life. During his periods of mental illness, he tended to associate St Ursula with Rose La Touche, a young woman for whom he nurtured an obsessive love. Today these paintings are displayed in the Accademia Gallery, Venice; they represent a further point of contact between the venerable city of the sea and this museum perched on a hill on the edge of Sheffield.

A manuscript case is visible in this photograph. It performs its function of preservation by keeping its contents behind glass, whilst ensuring the open pages can be perused. Ruskin indicated that students might earn the right to special kinds of access to the Museum's treasures. In his 1876 report on the purchase of the mineral cabinet, he explains that 'Permission to handle and examine them [the minerals] at ease will be eventually given, as a moral and mineralogical prize, to the men who attain a certain proficiency in the two sciences of Mineralogy and Behaviour'.[32] Presumably, the same instructions applied to the Museum's collection of precious manuscripts, amongst which were included a lectionary of the thirteenth century, a large manuscript Bible, and an illuminated Missal Album of Lady Diana de Croy (sixteenth century).

Other Exhibits

From 'Extension, View 3', we move to 'Other Exhibits', where important items are displayed that do not appear in the Victorian photographs. These include Ruskin's *Upper Part of the Figure of St George, after Carpaccio* (1872), a watercolour detail of Carpaccio's vision of St George in the Scuola di San Giorgio degli Schiavoni, Venice. Also notable is a photograph of one of the great palaces on the Grand Canal, *Palazzo Detto Ca Doro (The Ca' d'Oro)*, photographed by Giovanni Battista Brusa. A modern photograph of the building sits beside it, registering changes in the configuration of windows.

Consider, also, this hand-coloured lithograph on paper entitled *Common Scoter Duck* (c. 1840-1844) (figure 12), from *Birds of America* by John James Audubon (1785–1851). The plate comes from the T. C. Eyton Collection, which Ruskin bought for the Museum. The Eyton Collection contains almost 7000 hand-coloured prints and watercolour illustrations of birds by John and Elizabeth Gould, Audubon, Edward Lear and others. Apart from its 'truthful' representation of birds in their habitat, Ruskin might have appreciated the way it shows nature in miniature. Audubon's waves have the quality of a mountain range, and are comparable to the forms Ruskin captured in his watercolour, *The Matterhorn from the Moat of the Riffelhorn* (1849) (also filed under 'Other

Figure 12. John James Audubon (1785–1851), *'Common Scoter Duck'*, plate from *Birds of America*, Hand-coloured lithograph on paper, c. 1840-1844, Collection of the Guild of St George, Museums Sheffield

Exhibits'). Audubon's illustrations continue to be appreciated. On 7 December 2010, the *Guardian* reported that a copy of his *Birds of America* was sold at Sotheby's for £7.3 million.

'Exterior' View

Having seen the interior displays, we are in a position to explore the building's environs. The page marked 'Exterior' is part of the online museum because Ruskin was committed to an extra-mural conception of what a museum might be. He did not see its role as confined to the assemblage of works within a confined interior space. The built environment of the area, its industries, and its 'Alpine' setting, were meant to enter into dialogue with the disparate objects assembled inside. The Collection, and the fresh air, would readjust the perspective of visitors, making them see the views and themselves in a new way.

Hotspots on the 'Exterior' page serve two functions. Those placed on the building provide ways of exploring the wider physical context of the Museum. This is achieved primarily by 'filling in the gaps' between the historic photographs, and the rest of the structure. Modern pictures of the interior are used to further this purpose, providing an opportunity to consider points of change and continuity. In the upper rooms, an original fireplace has survived. A modern photograph shows the view from the windows as it appears today. A hotspot tagging the porch gives access to photographs of the hallway and the cellar. A further hotspot links to modern views of the kitchen, and includes information on surviving interior features. The ground-floor room (right-hand side) is especially significant because it is the most likely location of the original exhibition room ('Interior' view).

The room retains Victorian wood panelling in the window bays, and some plaster moulding (possibly post-dating the period of the Museum). Wooden windows have been replaced by PVC. The mantelpiece and fireplace have been removed. It is nevertheless illuminating to see those parts of the room that are not visible in the Victorian photograph, including its view on to the grounds.

Other hotspots in the 'Exterior' view are designed to evoke the Museum's built and natural environment. Clicking on the area immediately in front of the cottage opens a page devoted to views across the valley from the grounds.

Reconstructing historic views with complete accuracy is impossible, so the approach is to achieve an approximation. The Edwardian postcard included on this web page (figure 14) postdates the Museum, and the vantage point is

Downstairs Room

Showing interior in July 2009.

Chimney Breast, Downstairs Room, July 2009, copyright Marcus Waithe, 2009, taken with kind permission of John Smith, landlord of Ruskin House

Location

This room is served by a hallway door, situated on the east side wall just beyond the porch area.

It is the most likely location of the 'Interior' gallery photograph, although this has not been established beyond doubt.

Dimensions

The room measures 386 cm (depth) x 361 cm (frontal width). It is 275 cm in height.

The chimney breast is positioned on the south wall. It measures 143 cm across, with alcoves on either side measuring 106 cm and 112 cm. The left-hand alcove is 10.5 cm deep, and the right-hand, 13 cm.

Copyright Marcus Waithe, 2009; with thanks to John Smith, landlord of Ruskin House

Enlarge Image

The room has two large windows, one positioned in the west side wall, and the other at the front (see photograph). The window at the west side is 113 cm in width, and the north window is 110 cm in width. The door to the room measures 85 cm across.

Surviving Victorian Features

The room retains Victorian wood panelling in the window bays, and some plaster moulding (possibly post-dating the time of the Museum).

Wooden windows have been replaced by PVC. The mantelpiece and fireplace have been removed.

Figure 13. 'Downstairs Room', _Ruskin at Walkley_

Museum Surroundings and Views

The Museum stood on a generous plot of land, where fruit trees grew. From here, and especially from the upper windows, it enjoyed views over the Rivelin Valley and the Loxley Valley.

Enlarge Image

The Rivelin Valley was not free of industrial activity at that time. It had long been a centre for knife grinders, who used the river water to power mill stones. The derelict cottages and grinding mechanisms still found along the river testify to their activities. But such small scale industry did not interfere with Ruskin's impression of the valley as a pastoral scene.

'Afternoon Stroll from Sheffield', a sketch from 'St. George's Museums', *Pall Mall Gazette*, 14 May 1886

The view from the Museum reminded Ruskin of Alpine scenery, a source of childhood wonder as well as a subject of study in his art criticism. The effect was not exclusively visual: the fresh air blowing in from the Derbyshire hills ensured that the Museum's visitors would breathe a different atmosphere.

He described the 'beautiful scenery' in the Museum's locality, and included lines from a poem about the Rivelin Valley:

Figure 14. Detail of 'Old View of Rivelin Valley from Bole Hills', *Ruskin at Walkley*

different; but it achieves the desired effect in showing the appearance of the hillside before it was heavily developed. The other image is a contemporary sketch, published originally in *The Pall Mall Gazette* to accompany the report of a visiting journalist. The emphasis is not only on the idyllic atmosphere, but also on the desirability of beholding it; two figures recline on the hillside evidently enjoying a reward for their 'Afternoon Stroll'. A separate page shows a sketch of 'neighbouring cottages', in which Cook and Wedderburn report that 'pilgrims from distant cities' would stay for extended periods of study.[33]

A similar approach is taken to the Museum's built environment. Given the number of Victorian buildings still standing in the area, it is helpful to be reminded of what changes have occurred. One hotspot to the right of the Museum provides a sense of this.

Walkley Hall was the Museum's most imposing neighbour. The Sheffield Local Studies Library indicates that it was 'probably built by William Rawson in 1600', and that it 'was demolished in 1926 to make way for the present housing estate'.[34] The housing estate stands on Heavygate Road, a street that leads steeply uphill from Bole Hill Road to Crookes. The Sheffield Local Studies Library indicates that 'Heavygate Road was once a narrow lane and was known locally as Dark Lane'. Bole Hill Road was a rural lane in the 1880s,

Walkley Hall, Heavygate Road, 1900 [Image y01662 from the collections in Sheffield Local Studies Library, used with kind permission]

Image s05904 from the collections in Sheffield Local Studies Library, used with kind permission

Enlarge Image

Bole Hill Road ran behind the Museum. Although not exactly contemporary, these photographs of local buildings provide an indication the area's atmosphere.

Walkley Hall

A notable local building was Walkley Hall. The Sheffield Local Studies Library indicates that the Hall was 'probably built by William Rawson in 1600', and that it 'was demolished in 1926 to make way for the present housing estate'.

The new housing estate stands on Heavygate Road, a street that leads steeply uphill from Bole Hill Road. The Sheffield Local Studies Library indicates that 'Heavygate Road was once a narrow lane and was known locally as Dark Lane'.

The photograph on the right shows the imposing structure of Bole Hill Primary School. It is still standing, though now in different use. It was built by the Sheffield School Board in 1896 and is Grade II listed.

Although postdating the removal of the Museum from Walkley by six years, it serves as an indication of the rapid development occurring in the area. It would eventually stand sixty metres along the road from Ruskin House, on the opposite side of the street. The photograph is not dated, but is likely to be Edwardian.

Figure 15. Detail of 'Bole Hill Road and Local Buildings', *Ruskin at Walkley*

and it ran behind the St George's Museum. The photograph on the right of the web page shows the even larger edifice of Bole Hill Primary School. Still standing, though now in different use, the School was built by the Sheffield School Board in 1896 and is Grade II listed. Although postdating the removal of the Museum from Walkley by six years, it serves as an indication of the rapid development occurring in the area. It would eventually stand sixty metres away from Ruskin House, on the opposite side of the street.

Problems of Method

In the course of designing and building this resource, a number of issues arose regarding the proper method of 'reconstruction'.[35] The first of these concerned the labelling of exhibits. The original visitors to the Museum had to make do with an incomplete catalogue and patchy labels. The labels that survive state only the artist and title. These deficiencies found ample compensation in the presence of the Museum's hospitable curator. An obituary of Swan suggests that listening to him was 'like reading a few pages of Ruskin', because he 'used to take as much pains with those who could not appreciate what they saw as he would with a distinguished visitor'.[36] Viewers of the website do not receive the benefit of Swan's inside knowledge, though modern captions and detailed item descriptions are an attempt to make up for this. As one would expect of an accessible museum resource, prior knowledge is not taken for granted, and the tone is explanatory. In this respect, the 'reconstruction' is self-evidently something new; it avoids slavish reassembly in the interests of communicating with a modern audience. A further complication relates to the state of the displays in the three views of the Museum Extension. The movement from one view to another suggests the exploration of a continuous space; but certain discrepancies complicate the effect. In each of the three 'Extension' views, Ruskin's watercolour, *Santa Maria della Spina, Pisa* is present and facing the camera. Its omnipresence might suggest that the photographs were taken on different occasions, and that the painting happened to be in a new position each time. More likely, the photographer simply turned the painting round to create a pleasing and complete composition. There is a sense, in other words, that the room has been 'dressed' to please the camera. The same might be said of the 'Interior' view, where unframed works are propped in a seemingly temporary arrangement, ensuring that as many exhibits are fitted into the frame as possible. These considerations remind us that the photographs record a temporary stage, and that this stage is not wholly continuous across the individual images. Such features are reminders of the difficulties involved in interpreting photographic evidence. Problems are also posed by objects that are now either missing, unidentified, or sold. The centrepiece of the 'Interior' view is a painting that has disappeared from the Collection, William Small's watercolour *The Shipwreck* (1880). The most valuable painting in the collection was Verrocchio's *The Madonna Adoring the Christ Child* (*The Ruskin Madonna*). Sold by the Guild to the National Gallery of Scotland in 1975, its absence creates symbolic problems. Ruskin's insistence on Verrocchio's status as a 'worker in iron' formed a link with his target audience that the painting continues to evoke. The Guild has approached this difficulty in a Ruskinian spirit, by commissioning a copy and exhibiting it in The Ruskin Collection; for the website, a solution lies in the inclusion of a link to the original on the website of the National Gallery of Scotland. In this way, the reconstruction evokes not simply a connection with the past, but also the discontinuous nature of collections generally, the instability in what at first seems fixed and secure.

Future Developments

Items continue to be added to the Collection. One recent acquisition is an oil painting by J. W. Bunney, depicting the *Porta della Carta of the Ducal Palace* in Venice. It was bought by the Guild in 2010 to complement the works by Bunney already on display. In November 2011 William Small's painting, *The Shipwreck* was re-discovered in the vaults of the Graves Gallery in Sheffield. The website now displays a modern colour image of that work where before there was a blank. Never entirely static, or merely a memorial to Ruskin's life, the Collection remains, as it was at its inception, a working resource. It would be difficult, all the same, to understand its contents without some knowledge of its origins at Walkley, and of the displays that Swan contrived to fit into his cramped cottage interior. *Ruskin at Walkley* has been established to promote an awareness of that setting. It is hoped that fresh features will gradually be added, and that this new form of electronic accessibility will combine with the older forms Ruskin cultivated, to attract the attention of a new generation of visitors, students, and researchers. An electronic visitors' book was recently established, to continue the tradition established by the visitors' books kept at the Museum for the period, 1880-1891. There are also plans to digitise these original volumes, allowing modern visitors to see the names and addresses of their Victorian predecessors.

Marcus Waithe
2014
Magdalene College, Cambridge

Notes

1. Ruskin, 'The Guild of St. George. The Master's Report: 1881', in *The Library Edition of the Works of John Ruskin*, ed. by E. T. Cook and Alexander Wedderburn, 39 vols (London: George Allen, 1903-12), 30, pp. 31-42 (p. 39). Given as *Works* in subsequent references.

2. Ruskin, 'Letter 56 (August 1875)', *Fors Clavigera*, in *Works*, 28, p. 395.

3. Ruskin 'Letter 56 (August 1875)', *Fors Clavigera*, in *Works*, 28, pp. 383-401 (p. 395).

4. Ruskin, 'The Puppet Show', in *Works*, 2, p. xxxiii.

5. Ruskin, 'Letter 26 (February 1873)', *Fors Clavigera*, in *Works*, 27, pp. 473-488 (p. 475).

6. Ruskin, 'Letter 5 (May 1871)', *Fors Clavigera*, in *Works*, 27, pp. 79-97 (p. 95).

7. Ruskin, 'Letter 5 (May 1871)', *Fors Clavigera*, in *Works*, 27, pp. 79-97 (p. 95).

8. Ruskin, Letter 2 (February 1871) *Fors Clavigera*, in *Works*, 27, p. 28.

9. Ruskin, 'The Guild of St George. The Master's Report: 1879', in *Works*, 30, pp. 15-28 (p. 17).

10. Ruskin, 'General Statement Explaining the Nature and Purposes of St George's Guild' (1882), in *Works*, 30, pp. 45-59 (p. 52).

11. Ruskin, 'General Statement Explaining the Nature and Purposes of St George's Guild' (1882), in *Works*, 30, pp. 45-59 (p. 52).

12. Reported in 'Visit of Prince Leopold to the Walkley Museum (1879)', in *Works*, 30, pp. 311-314 (p. 311).

13. Ruskin, 'Circular Respecting Memorial Studies of St. Mark's, Venice, Now in Progress under Mr. Ruskin's Direction', in *Works*, 24, pp. 412-416 (p. 412).

14. Ruskin, 'Letter in *The Times*, March 6, 1883', in *Works*, 30, pp. 316-317 (p. 317).

15. Edward Bradbury, 'A Visit to Mr Ruskin's Museum', *Magazine of Art*, December 1879, pp. 57-60

16. Anon., 'The Ruskin Museum at Sheffield', *The Daily Graphic*, 15 April 1890, p. 5.

17. Ruskin, 'General Statement Explaining the Nature and Purposes of St George's Guild' (1882), in *Works*, 30, pp. 45-59 (p. 52).

18. Ruskin, Letter 88 (March 1880), in *Fors Clavigera*, in *Works*, 29, pp. 381-397 (p. 397).

19. Ruskin, 'Discussion and Letters upon the Proposal to Build a new Museum', in *Works*, 30, pp. 314-327 (p. 315).

20. For more information on the history of the Ruskin Museum, including its subsequent home at Meersbrook, Reading University, and Norfolk Street, see Janet Barnes, *Ruskin in Sheffield* (The Ruskin Gallery/Sheffield Arts and Museum Department, 1985; new edition, Museums Sheffield, 2011). Barnes's book is an important source for the account provided on the website.

21. Catherine W. Morley, *John Ruskin: Late Work 1870-1890: The Museum and Guild of St George: An Educational Experiment* (London and New York: Garland Press, 1984), p. 75.

22. *Sheffield Illustrated: Views and Portraits which have Appeared in the Sheffield Weekly Telegraph During the Year 1884* (W. C. Leng & Co., 1884).

23. Volume introduction, *Works*, 30, p. xlv.

24. Ruskin, *The Stones of Venice*, in *Works*, 10, p. 201.

25. Ruskin, 'Notes on The Louvre', in *Works*, 12, pp. 448-456 (p. 452).

26. Uncatalogued invoice, 15 December 1882, Ruskin Gallery Archive.

27. Uncatalogued invoice, 15 December 1882, Ruskin Gallery Archive.

28. Volume introduction, *Works*, 10, p. lxiii.

[29] Ruskin, *Ariadne Florentina*, in *Works*, 22, p. 476.

[30] Ruskin, 'General Statement Explaining the Nature and Purposes of St George's Guild' (1882), in *Works*, 30, pp. 45-59 (p. 55).

[31] 'Catalogue of the St George's Museum as now Arranged in Meersbrook Park, Sheffield', *Works*, 30, pp. 187-293 (p. 188).

[32] Ruskin', 'Letter 69 (September 1876)', *Fors Clavigera*, in *Works*, 28, pp. 687-711 (p. 702).

[33] Volume introduction, *Works*, 30, p. xliii.

[34] Sheffield Library Service: image text for 'Walkley Hall', Ref No. y01662, Picture Sheffield <http://www.picturesheffield.com> [accessed 24 January 2011] (para. 1 of 1).

[35] For a fuller discussion of these issues, see Marcus Waithe, 'John Ruskin and the Idea of Museum', forthcoming in *Disseminating Ruskin*, ed. by Brian Maidment and Keith Hanley' (Ashgate).

[36] 'The "Faithful Steward" of the Ruskin Museum. (By One Who Knew Him.)', *The Pall Mall Gazette*, 2 April 1889, p. 2.